BACKYARD BIRDING FOR KIDS

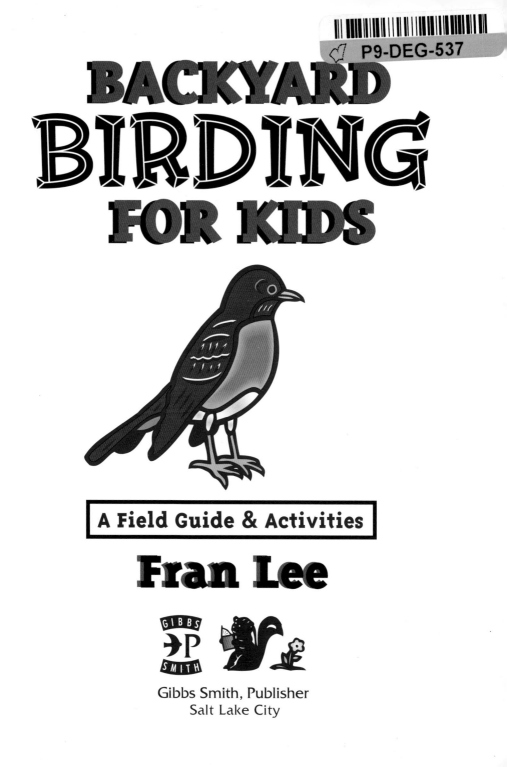

A Field Guide & Activities

Fran Lee

Gibbs Smith, Publisher
Salt Lake City

For my uncle, M. W. Newman, with love.
He was a magnificent observer, superior reporter,
friend of animals, and friend of mine.

● ● ●

First Edition

14 13   7 6

Text and Illustrations © 2005 by Fran Lee

Published by
Gibbs Smith, Publisher
P.O. Box 667
Layton, Utah 84041

Orders: (1-800) 748-5439
www.gibbs-smith.com

Designed by Fran Lee
Manufactured in Hong Kong in July 2013 by Paramount Printing Company Ltd.

Note: Some of the activities suggested in this book require adult supervision. Children
and their guardians should always use common sense and good judgment in playing,
cooking, and making crafts. The publisher and author assume no responsibility for any
damages or injuries incurred while performing any of the activities in this book; neither
are they responsible for the results of these projects.

Library of Congress Cataloging-in-Publication Data
Lee, Fran.
Backyard birding for kids : a field guide and activities / written and
illustrated by Fran Lee.—1st ed.
p. cm.
ISBN 10:1-58685-411-9
ISBN 13:978-1-58685-411-9
I. Bird watching—Juvenile literature.
I. Title. QL677.5.L424 2005
598'.072'34—dc22
2004021361

CONTENTS

YOU ARE A BIRD-WATCHER !

D o you enjoy watching the birds outside your window? If you have spent time watching the same birds every day, you may have noticed a few things. A House Sparrow hopping around on the roof with bits of string and dried grass in its bill is building a nest—probably in the gutters! A Robin splashing around in the birdbath is taking a bath. A Blue Jay visiting your backyard bird feeder is ready to eat. Do you repeat the Chickadee's song when you hear it? Does seeing a Sharp-Shinned Hawk soaring through your backyard make your spine tingle? Guess what? You are a bird-watcher!

Bird-Friendly Backyard

By taking a closer look, we can learn something from every bird we see. Look out your favorite window or cruise around your neighborhood. What birds do you see? You can attract many species of birds to your backyard by making it bird-friendly. Put up bird feeders, add a birdbath, grow plants and flowers that birds will enjoy. Provide nesting areas by putting up nesting boxes or birdhouses. If you live in an apartment, ask a parent if you can put up a window feeder. Take care of your feeders by keeping them clean and full of delicious bird food. Refill the birdbath often with clean, fresh water. Enjoy watching and identifying all the birds that pay a visit to your bird-friendly backyard.

Where to Look

You can go bird-watching anywhere. You could sit in your own backyard, take a walk in the city park or a hike in the woods, stand quietly at the edge of a marsh or in an open field, take your binoculars to the beach. Where are birds' favorite places? Visit the wildlife refuges, national parks, and bird sanctuaries in your area.

Birds are everywhere. Look up in the sky and what do you see? In the spring you will see birds migrating north, and in the fall you'll see flocks flying south for the winter. Many birds are busiest during the early morning, so this is a good time to plan an outing. Some birds, such as Ducks and Hawks, can be spotted throughout the day, and other birds, like Owls, are more active at dusk and in the evening. What kinds of birds are most commonly seen or least commonly seen in your area?

When bird-watching, take your time, walk slowly and quietly. Survey the surroundings, notice every detail and every movement. Sit in one place very quietly for ten minutes to half an hour. If you are lucky, you may see some of our fine feathered friends enjoying the great outdoors with you. Record your findings by keeping a record in your Bird-Watching Notebook (see page 53). Now you're really bird-watching!

What Do We Need?

Not much! The two most important things you will need for bird-watching are a good pair of eyes and a good pair of ears. It is also helpful to have the items shown on page 7.

Bird Field Guide Books

Over 700 known species of birds build their nests in North America and scientists are discovering more all the time. Bird field guide books have maps that show where in the country or region a species of a bird lives. They also have information about the behavior and appearance of individual birds, and an index to help you find what you are looking for. Most importantly, they have illustrations or photos of each type of bird.

Binoculars

It is important to take good care of your binoculars and make sure they have a comfortable neck strap, and that the neck strap is where it should be: around your neck! (You do not want to drop them or lose them.)

◆ After spotting a bird, keep your eyes on it. Do not look away, or you might lose track of it.

◆ Find a focal point (a patch of red leaves, for instance) that stands out and is close to the bird that you have spotted. Then raise the binoculars to your eyes and look for the focal point; find it, and the bird should be nearby.

WHAT YOU NEED

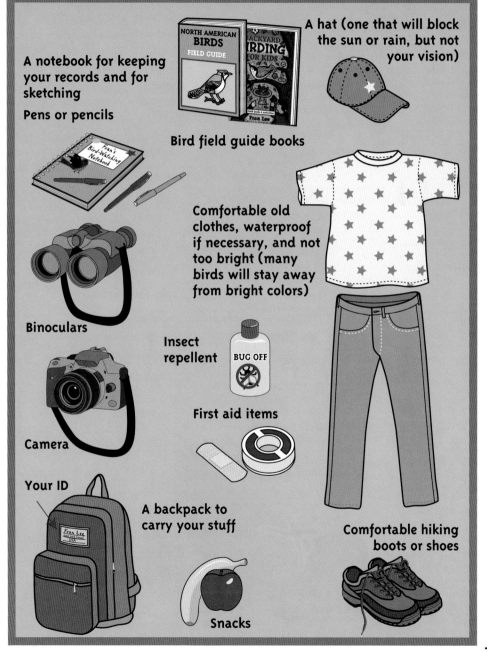

A notebook for keeping your records and for sketching

Pens or pencils

Bird field guide books

NORTH AMERICAN BIRDS FIELD GUIDE

BACKYARD BIRDING FOR KIDS

Fran Lee

A hat (one that will block the sun or rain, but not your vision)

Comfortable old clothes, waterproof if necessary, and not too bright (many birds will stay away from bright colors)

Binoculars

Insect repellent

BUG OFF

First aid items

Camera

Your ID

A backpack to carry your stuff

Snacks

Comfortable hiking boots or shoes

Name That Bird!

Species

A species of bird is a group of birds that are alike in the way they look, behave, and sound. These birds breed with each other successfully. Each species of bird has a common name and a Latin name.

Common name

The common name is the one we are most familiar with. Chickadees are named after the "chicka-dee-dee-dee" song that they sing. The Black-Capped Chickadee is named for its song and its black crown. Many birds are named after an outstanding feature, such as the Red-Winged Blackbird. Some birds are named after the place where they were discovered. Some ornithologists have named birds after friends, relatives, or employers. For instance, Anna's Hummingbird was named after a friend of the zoologist who first discovered the bird.

Latin name

The Latin name is the bird's scientific name. The Yellow Warbler's Latin name is *Dendroica petechia*. Sometime birds have more than one common name, depending on where you are in the world; so, common names can be confusing. But Latin names stay the same and help bird-watchers worldwide identify and classify bird species.

Family

A family of birds is a group of different species that are a lot alike in many ways, but they do not interbreed. For instance, the Fox Sparrow and the White-Crowned Sparrow are two different species in the Sparrow family.

What Do We Look For?

Take time to watch the bird. What is it doing? Is it alone or in a group?

Field Marks

Field marks are distinctive marks on a bird that help us identify one species from another. Think of these as visual clues.

FIELD MARKS

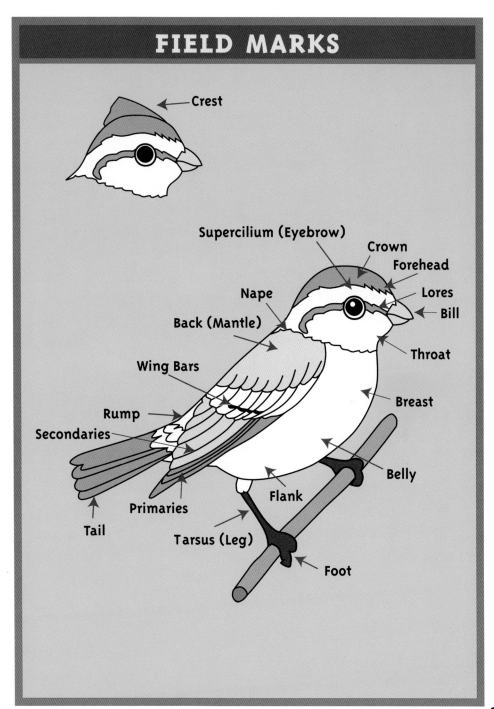

Crest

Supercilium (Eyebrow)

Crown

Forehead

Nape

Lores

Back (Mantle)

Bill

Wing Bars

Throat

Rump

Breast

Secondaries

Primaries

Belly

Tail

Flank

Tarsus (Leg)

Foot

A Bird's Body

Observing the different parts of a bird will help you identify it, and you will discover details about its daily life. What kind of food does this bird eat? Look at its bill: is it sharp, or round and flat? Does the bird swim or does it perch in a tree? Look at its feet: are they webbed? What size is the bird? Does it have unusual eye markings, or colorful wing or tail feathers?

Feet and Legs

Birds have scales on their feet and legs, a link to the reptiles that were their prehistoric ancestors.

Wading birds and shorebirds, like Herons and Cranes, have long legs that help them wade into the water to find their dinner. Swimming birds have webbed feet that work as paddles, and strong legs that help them dive and swim.

Birds that perch on branches, like Sparrows, have one strong claw in the back and three front claws. They use their back claw to grab the branch.

Birds of prey (see page 23), like Owls and Eagles, have strong, sharp claws called talons, for catching and holding their prey.

Bills and Beaks

A bird's bill (or beak) is like a tool. It is shaped in a way that best helps it get its food. Birds of prey, like Eagles and Hawks, have strong, sharp, short, curved beaks for tearing the flesh of their victims. Parrots and Parakeets have beaks that are hinged like a nutcracker for cracking seeds. Herons and Cranes have long, thin, pointed beaks shaped like spears for hunting fish in the water. Hummingbirds have very thin, delicate bills that they use as tiny straws to suck the nectar out of their favorite flowers.

Feathers

"Plumage" is the name of all the feathers that cover a bird's body. Birds are the only animals that have feathers.

The hollow base of the feather is called a quill; this is the part that sticks into the bird's skin. The middle strip that grows from the quill is called a shaft. More than 600 pairs of barbs grow out from the center of the shaft, fitting together like a zipper to make a smooth surface called the vane. If you rub the vane the wrong way, you will "ruffle" a feather.

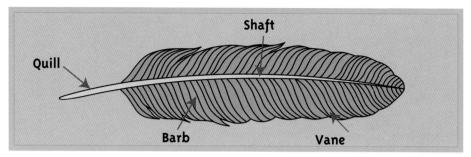

Feathers keep a bird's body warm and protect it from harsh weather. Though they are light, feathers are very strong and help the bird to fly. An adult bird has strong flying feathers on its wings and tail. Its soft body feathers, called "down," can be used as soft, warm nest lining for the comfort of newly hatched baby birds.

Baby birds may start life with soft downy feathers, or they may start out pink and naked and grow their down in a few days. As they grow up, they grow their flying feathers. A bird "molts" once, or sometimes twice, a year. Molting is when a bird loses its old feathers and grows new ones. A bird takes care of its feathers by "preening" with its beak, using an oil from a gland at the base of its tail.

Wings and Tails

A bird's wing has three main types of feathers. If you think of a wing like an arm and a hand, the longest feathers are the "hand," and these are called primaries. The "arm" has secondaries that grow over the primaries. Then there are the wing coverts, which are smaller, shorter feathers that grow under and over the longer feathers.

Bird Songs

Use your ears as well as your eyes. Is that bird singing its little heart out? Do you recognize the bird song and know what species it belongs to? Birds make all sorts of noises! From the flap of their wings to the trill in their tune, bird sounds are another way you can identify birds. Birds sing, call, and screech with alarm. Some birds even mimic other birds' voices. Male birds may sing to attract a mate, or to establish their territory. Birds communicate with calls and chatter. They may be saying, "Hey, I'm over here and so is the food!" or "Watch out, there's a big cat coming this way!"

Knowing a bird's song can help you identify it. Listen to recordings of bird songs before you take a hike. These are available at the library, bookstore, or birding center. You may want to take a tape recorder with you and make your own tapes.

Bird-Watching Etiquette

Bird-watching is fun. To make it fun for everyone, it is important to respect these 3 things:

◆ **The Birds:** Watch and observe, but do not disturb or touch.

◆ **The Environment:** Do not litter, disturb, or destroy in any way.

◆ **Fellow Birders:** Respect other bird-watchers' space. If you see and want to identify a bird first, try not to yell out its name—give others a chance to find it and identify it for themselves.

Birds Are Everywhere

We've been looking at birds all our lives. Aren't we lucky to share our environment with these interesting, beautiful, and amazing friends?

CITY BIRDS

Do Pigeons poke around on the roof of the buildings next door to you? Are there flocks of Geese and Ducks that visit the pond in your city park? Have you ever watched a Hawk build its nest in the under-structure of a huge bridge?

If you are visiting or live in the city, you will have the pleasure of watching a variety of amazing birds. If you have a bird-friendly yard, some birds may visit it all year-round, and others may come and go with the seasons. You might think that cities or urban areas are only full of buildings, cars, and people, but cities have many habitats for birds.

The popular birds pictured in this chapter spend some or all of their time in a city or urban habitat. Be on the lookout for them as you take a walk in the park, visit a garden or nature spot, or go down to the water's edge by the river or lake.

American Robin

- About 10 inches long
- Member of Thrush family
- Male is brighter than female
- Young have black spots on tan breast
- Eggs are pale blue color
- First bird to sing in the morning
- Likes to eat earthworms, bugs, vegetables, and fruit
- Likes to take baths in birdbaths

Doves

Rock Dove

- From 12 to 14 inches long
- Most common bird in North America, also known as Pigeon
- Very tame
- Takes over rooftops and ledges; some people consider it a pest
- Drinks by sucking water

Mourning Dove

- From 10 to 12 inches long
- Slimmer than the Rock Dove
- Walks instead of hopping and bobs head while walking
- Considered very affectionate; its love song sounds like mournful cooing

Ruby-Throated Hummingbird

- ❀ About 3½ inches long
- ❀ Heart beats 615 times per second, and wings beat 75 times per second
- ❀ Can fly at the speed of 30 miles per hour
- ❀ Its nest is a tiny cup just 1 inch wide and 1 inch deep, made of buds and plants held together by the silk of spiders and caterpillars
- ❀ Female lays 1 or 2 little white eggs the size of a pea
- ❀ Female does not have ruby throat patch

Black-Capped Chickadee

- ❀ Plump and small, about 5 inches long
- ❀ Known and named for its familiar call: *"Chicka dee-dee-dee-dee"*
- ❀ Likes to eat suet, sunflower seeds, pumpkin seeds, and nut kernels
- ❀ Turns complete somersaults in search of food
- ❀ When eggs hatch, a mated pair works together to feed their young

Jays

Blue Jay

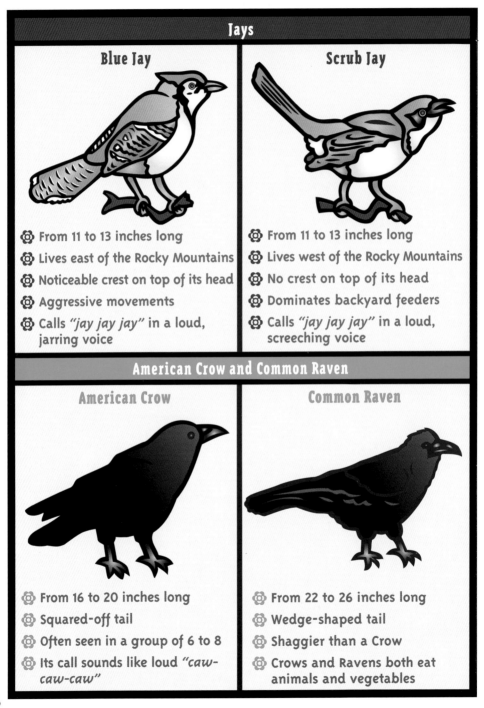

- From 11 to 13 inches long
- Lives east of the Rocky Mountains
- Noticeable crest on top of its head
- Aggressive movements
- Calls *"jay jay jay"* in a loud, jarring voice

Scrub Jay

- From 11 to 13 inches long
- Lives west of the Rocky Mountains
- No crest on top of its head
- Dominates backyard feeders
- Calls *"jay jay jay"* in a loud, screeching voice

American Crow and Common Raven

American Crow

- From 16 to 20 inches long
- Squared-off tail
- Often seen in a group of 6 to 8
- Its call sounds like loud *"caw-caw-caw"*

Common Raven

- From 22 to 26 inches long
- Wedge-shaped tail
- Shaggier than a Crow
- Crows and Ravens both eat animals and vegetables

16

House Finch

- 5 to 6 inches long
- Female is brown with a streaked underbelly
- Short, wide beak for cracking seeds
- On the East Coast, birds are darker than on the West Coast
- Has a long, forked tail
- In the early 1940s, Finches were sold in pet shops, but a ban on selling them as pets led bird dealers to release them into the wild

House Sparrow

- 5 to 6 inches long
- Was brought here from Europe in the 1850s
- Though called a Sparrow, it is more like a Finch
- Females and their young are streaked with light and dark brown feathers on top of their heads, backs, wings, and tails
- Likes to eat insects and seeds from weeds
- Some people consider it a pest

Eastern Bluebird

- About 6 inches long
- Member of Thrush family
- Builds its nest in the hollow of a tree; uses old nesting holes of Woodpeckers
- Can be attracted to feeders by offering brightly colored berries or a dish of mealworms
- Three species of Bluebird in North America: the Eastern Bluebird, the Western Bluebird, the Mountain Bluebird

Northern Cardinal

- About 8 to 9 inches long
- Female is muted brown, though she may have some red on her crest
- It is the only red bird that has a crest
- Voice sounds like a series of loud, clear whistles, *"wheat wheat what-cheer what-cheer"*
- Male uses a song to establish his territory
- The St. Louis baseball team is named after the red Cardinal

FEED THE BIRDS!

Feeders

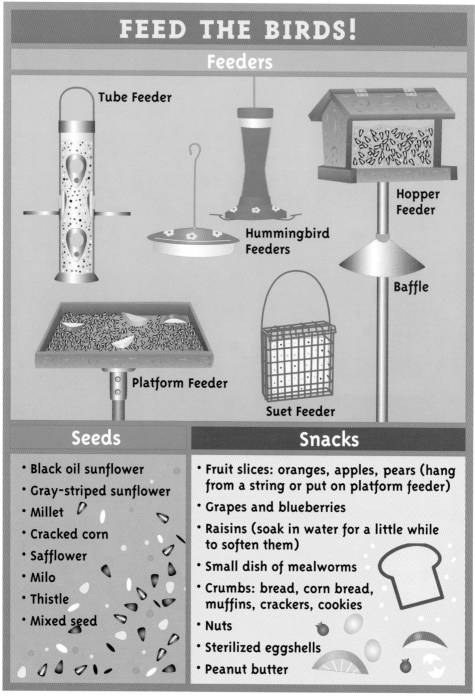

Tube Feeder

Hummingbird Feeders

Hopper Feeder

Baffle

Platform Feeder

Suet Feeder

Seeds

- Black oil sunflower
- Gray-striped sunflower
- Millet
- Cracked corn
- Safflower
- Milo
- Thistle
- Mixed seed

Snacks

- Fruit slices: oranges, apples, pears (hang from a string or put on platform feeder)
- Grapes and blueberries
- Raisins (soak in water for a little while to soften them)
- Small dish of mealworms
- Crumbs: bread, corn bread, muffins, crackers, cookies
- Nuts
- Sterilized eggshells
- Peanut butter

PINECONE BIRD FEEDER

Makes 4 pinecone feeders

What you need:

Newspaper

5-pound bag birdseed

2 cups peanut butter

1 cup cornmeal

4 large pinecones (one per feeder)

4 pieces sturdy string or twine, cut into 2-foot lengths

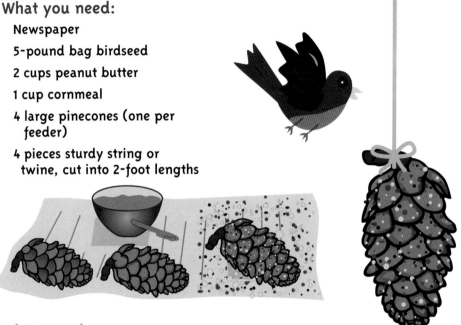

What you do:

1. Cover work surface with newspaper.
2. Pour 2 to 3 cups of birdseed onto a large baking pan.
3. Using a spatula or wooden spoon, mix peanut butter and cornmeal together in a medium-sized bowl.
4. Using a butter knife, spread the mixture all over the pinecones. Be careful as you get it in all the layers of the cone—you don't want to break off any parts.
5. Roll each peanut butter–covered pinecone in the birdseed; the seeds will stick to the peanut butter. Shake the cone to get off any extra seeds.
6. Tie one end of your string to the top part of the pinecone.
7. Tie the other end of the string to a hook or nail outside where you can view it and where the birds have easy access to it.
8. When the birdseed spread is gone, you can "refill" the feeder by repeating these steps.

20

HUMMINGBIRD FEEDER

A Hummingbird feeder should be easy to clean, simple to use, and should not leak or drip. Many Hummingbird feeders have red parts because these birds are attracted to red. If your feeder does not have the color red anywhere, tie a red ribbon on it. Remember to clean and refill your feeder every 3 days.

To Make a Hummingbird Feeder:

Use a small glass jar as a Hummingbird feeder, by tying a wire around the lip of the jar and securing the jar to a pole or sturdy backing, like a fencepost or tree. Tie a red ribbon around the jar and fill it with nectar.

To Make Homemade Nectar:

4 cups boiling water

1 cup sugar

Have an adult help you pour the boiling water into a plastic pitcher or container. Add sugar. Stir until sugar dissolves, then let it cool. If you make extra, you can store it in the refrigerator until it is time to refill the feeder.

Plant a Hummingbird Garden:

Hummingbirds love the nectar in bell-shaped red, orange, pink, and purple flowers. These include bee balm, impatiens, carpet bugle, delphinium, gladioli, phlox, and sage.

THE SMALLEST BIRD  The *Bee Hummingbird*, found in Cuba, is about 2 inches long and weighs about $\frac{1}{15}$ of an ounce. Light as a feather and small as a bee!

WOODLAND BIRDS

Looking for birds in wooded areas works better when you follow these three rules:

1. Move quietly.
2. Use your ears.
3. Know the habitat.

If possible, walk on a trail instead of the forest ground. This keeps you from making noise by walking over leaves and branches. At first, you may think there are few birds in the woods, but take your time, stay in one place, scan all the levels of the forest. Some birds like to be high up in the trees, some like the middle branches, and others prefer to be near or on the ground.

Sometimes it is hard to see the birds in the trees because of the dense plants and leaves. This is why it is good to use your ears. You may be able to track a bird and identify it by its song or call. Watch birds that are singing or calling, remember their sound, and then later, connect what you've heard with what you've seen.

Many bird species have favorite trees or plants. Use your Bird-Watching Notebook (see page 53) to keep track of what trees and plants you see birds near, and you may be able to guess what kinds of birds you'll see at each habitat.

The season (time of year) and the weather also play an important role in when a bird species will live in forested areas. In this chapter, we will learn about some interesting birds you may see on your walk through the woods.

BIRDS OF PREY

Eagles, Falcons, Hawks, and Owls are "birds of prey." Birds of prey are also called "raptors." They are carnivores (meat eaters), and to survive, they kill and eat other animals, like small rodents, snakes, and small birds. Birds of prey have sharp, strong, hooked beaks that are used for killing and tearing flesh. The sharp, razor-like claws on their feet are called talons. These are used for grabbing and killing prey.

Downy Woodpecker

- 5 to 7 inches long
- Pecks 100 times a minute, making a loud *"tat-a-tat-tat"* sound
- Has 4 toes—2 point forward, 2 backward
- Spends most of its time climbing up tree trunks in a spiraling path
- Chops into tree bark with its beak
- Uses its long, sticky tongue to catch and eat insects, insect eggs, and larvae; likes sap, fruit, and seeds

Northern Flicker

- 10 to 13 inches long
- Its loud call sounds like *"wick wick wick"*
- When flying, its white rump is clearly in sight
- There are three kinds of Northern Flickers: the Yellow-Shafted Flicker in the East, the Red-Shafted Flicker in the West, and the Gilded Flicker in the Southwest
- The Red-Shafted and Gilded Flicker have a red mustache; the Yellow-Shafted Flicker has a black mustache

Sharp-Shinned Hawk

- 10 to 14 inches long, smallest Hawk in North America
- Part of a Hawk group called Accipiters
- Accipiters are Hawks characterized by their flight pattern—a series of short wing beats, and then a long glide
- Nicknamed "Sharpie"
- The Sharpie is a bird of prey and is the most common woodland Hawk in North America

Great Horned Owl

- 19 to 24 inches long
- Call is *"hoo, hoo, hoo"*
- A fierce bird of prey, it has been called the "Flying Tiger"
- You can tell it from other owls by its widely spaced ear tufts that look like little horns
- Rarely builds its own nest, preferring abandoned Hawk or Eagle nests
- The first primary feather on each wing has a jagged edge, allowing it to fly in silence

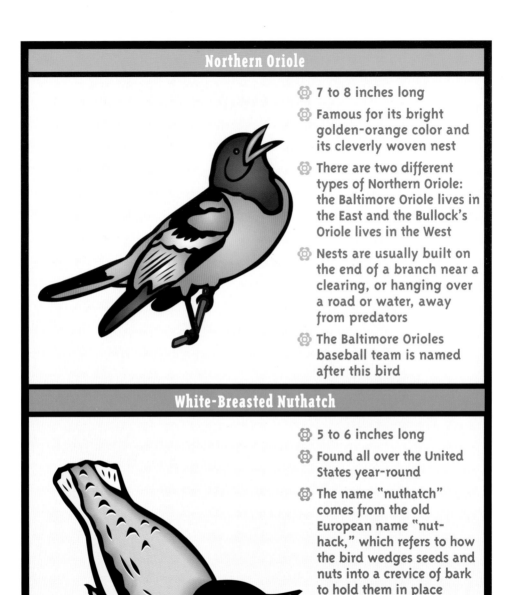

Northern Oriole

- 7 to 8 inches long
- Famous for its bright golden-orange color and its cleverly woven nest
- There are two different types of Northern Oriole: the Baltimore Oriole lives in the East and the Bullock's Oriole lives in the West
- Nests are usually built on the end of a branch near a clearing, or hanging over a road or water, away from predators
- The Baltimore Orioles baseball team is named after this bird

White-Breasted Nuthatch

- 5 to 6 inches long
- Found all over the United States year-round
- The name "nuthatch" comes from the old European name "nut-hack," which refers to how the bird wedges seeds and nuts into a crevice of bark to hold them in place while it hammers away with its chisel-like beak to crack them open
- Female is paler than the male, and their cap is more gray

NESTING BOXES and BIRDHOUSES

A nest gives birds protection from bad weather, a place to sleep, and a place to lay their eggs and raise a family. Some birds build a nest on the ground. Others make a cup- or bowl-shaped nest in a tree by weaving together little sticks, parts of plants, and bits of string and paper. Some birds choose a hole in a tree or another hollow space to build their nest.

Tips for Putting Up Birdhouses

◆ Put your box or house in a safe place. Trees are not great spots because predators can climb the trunk to get to the birdhouse. If you place your house on a pole, you may want to have a "baffle" beneath the box to discourage predators. A baffle is a type of guard that you put underneath the birdhouse to block any unwanted visitors. You can put these on bird feeders as well (see page 19).

◆ Clean out last year's nest stuff. Birds like a clean space to start a home.

◆ Make sure the home is warm, dry, and airy.

◆ Do not paint, stain, or shellac the inside of the box—leave it natural.

◆ The box should be the right size for the bird, and at least 6 x 6 x 6 inches. If you are purchasing or building a nesting box, it is best to research it or ask an expert what size box and entry hole is right for the birds you want to attract.

TED'S BIRD SHELF

Many birds, including Robins, Barn Swallows, Phoebes, and Great Horned Owls, prefer to nest on platform structures rather than enclosed spaces. You and your adult helper can make a bird shelf from scraps of wood. Hang it in a secure place and watch your new neighbor move in!

What you need:
- ¹/₂-inch thick plywood
- Hand or power saw
- Hammer
- 1¹/₂-inch finishing nails
- ¹/₂-inch screws
- Mirror plate

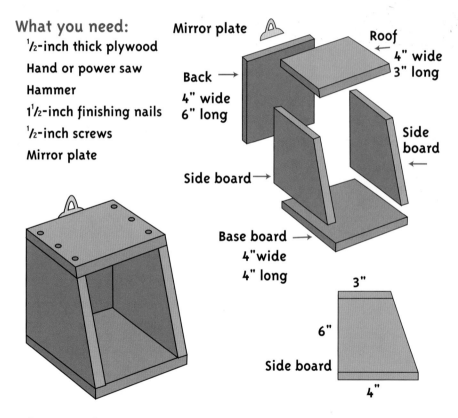

Mirror plate

Back →
4" wide
6" long

Roof
← 4" wide
3" long

Side board
←

Side board →

Base board →
4" wide
4" long

3"

6"

Side board

4"

What you do:
1. From the ¹/₂-inch thick plywood, cut 5 sections to the diagram's dimensions.
2. Using the finishing nails, attach the sections together as shown.
3. Attach a mirror plate behind the back section using the screws, and mount assembled bird shelf to a safe and secure structure.

A BEAUTIFUL NEST

During spring, it is a common sight to see birds collecting materials for their nests. They might gather strips of plants, dried grass, paper, pieces of fabric—whatever they can find. It's fun to contribute to the beauty of the nest by providing nesting materials.

What you need:
Colorful yarn, ribbon, or string

Scissors

What you do:

1. Cut yarn, ribbon, or string into strips approximately 2 to 4 inches long.

2. Place these strips around your yard and hang them on tree limbs and bushes.

3. Keep your eyes open. See a bright spot of color over there in those trees? That looks like a ribbon from your birthday party! Now it's part of that bird's nest! Cool!

 You can really make your parents happy by sweeping up any fur your pets have shed recently. If you take this fur and place it around your yard, it may be recycled by a bird and used to cushion the bottom of its nest!

COUNTRY BIRDS

Grasslands, open fields, alpine meadows, arctic tundra, and farmland all provide great opportunities for bird-watching because in these open areas birds are not as hidden as they are in the woods. Freshly plowed fields bring insects to the surface, and this attracts all kinds of hungry birds. Tall grass provides shelter, and in the fall and winter open fields provide food for many birds that may nest in other habitats. Stay close to hedges or the edge of the woods so you do not disturb or frighten the birds. In open fields you may be quite far from a bird, so don't forget your binoculars. You can even bird-watch while riding in a car. Keep an eye out for birds perching on telephone lines, poles, and fences. In this chapter, we will learn about some of the birds you may see while bird-watching in the country.

Northern Harrier

- 16 to 22 inches long
- It is a low-flying Hawk
- A bird of prey, its quick reflexes are used as elements of surprise when catching meals
- Because it searches for its prey over meadows and marshes, it was at one time called the Marsh Hawk
- Female is larger than the male
- Bold white patch of feathers at the base of its tail

American Kestrel

- 8 to 11 inches long, the smallest American Falcon
- Females are bigger than males
- A swift flyer, it hovers over open fields, scanning the ground for grasshoppers or small rodents, dropping swiftly down when it spots its target
- Females have reddish-brown wings; males have blue wings

Barn Owl

- 🏵 14 to 16 inches long
- 🏵 Has a blood-curdling scream
- 🏵 Lives all over the world; in the United States it lives in the open rural areas
- 🏵 Can also be found in urban areas; nesting boxes, provided by people in places like New York City, help keep the Barn Owl alive and well
- 🏵 Its central pectinate (comb-like) toenail used for preening (grooming)

Common Nighthawk

- 🏵 About 10 inches long
- 🏵 Misnamed: it is not a Hawk, but is a Nightjar; may be seen in the evening, but also active during the day
- 🏵 Does not build a nest; female lays eggs in a spot chosen with care (sometimes this may be on a rooftop of an office building)
- 🏵 Beak opens into a big mouth, perfect for catching flying insects
- 🏵 Sharp nasal voice sounds like *"peehk"*

Brown-Headed Cowbird

- 🌼 6 to 8 inches long
- 🌼 Member of the Blackbird family
- 🌼 Originally lived among herds of buffalo and cows on the Great Plains, living off the insects stirred up by the movement of the herds; needs open fields to find food
- 🌼 Female does not build her own nest, but lays eggs in the nests of other birds; these other birds will sometimes raise the baby Cowbird

American Goldfinch

- 🌼 4 to 5 inches long
- 🌼 Unusual flight pattern: looks like it is riding a roller coaster—flaps its wings and flies upward as fast as it can, then folds wings to its sides and glides down
- 🌼 Chatter sounds like it is saying *"potato-chips"*
- 🌼 Builds its nest in late summer when plants and weeds have gone to seed
- 🌼 Likes to eat thistle; loves this seed in backyard bird feeders

A SUNFLOWER GARDEN

Wild birds live outside where trees and flowers provide them with food, nesting spots, and shelter. An ideal backyard bird-friendly habitat should have trees, bushes, and lots of plants arranged in a natural and inviting way. Birds like to perch in trees and have room to fly. They like to hide in dead branches, old stumps, and discarded Christmas trees placed around the yard. Keep your backyard free of any chemical pesticides or fertilizers that could harm birds or other animals.

Sunflowers

Sunflower seeds are a favorite of seed-eating birds. There are many varieties of sunflowers, and birds like them all. The giant single-headed variety of sunflower is fun to grow, but you have to have some room because it grows very fast, and gets very big. If you live where you do not have a garden spot, you can grow sunflowers in pots on a ledge or porch. Make sure you have the right size pot for the flowers, room for them to grow, and lots of sun. Grow your sunflower seeds in full sun.

What you need:

Garden soil	Water
Mulch or peat	Garden spade
Sunflower seeds	Tall wooden stakes, one per plant
1 medium-sized planting pot per plant	Twine or string

What you do:

1. In early spring, fill each pot with a mixture of soil and mulch or peat. This soil mixture should be nice and damp.
2. Plant 4 seeds per pot, about 1 inch down from the surface, spaced evenly apart. Cover the seeds with soil and water. Set in a sunny place.
3. Soon tiny seedlings will begin to grow. Pull out three of these, leaving the largest. This one has the best chance of becoming the biggest and healthiest flower. If you are not going to transfer this plant into a garden, your sunflower should be very happy in its pot, in the sun.

4. If you are going to transplant the sunflower into your garden, choose a sunny spot that is large enough for your flower to grow. Make sure the spot has been weeded, and the soil has been turned and prepared with some natural fertilizer, peat, or mulch.

5. Dig holes for your plants 18 inches apart. The holes should be twice as big around as the bottom of the planting pot.

6. Carefully tip your plant out of its pot and settle it into the planting hole. Then fill the hole with soil. Water gently.

7. Push a wooden stake into the dirt to help support the sunflower if it grows very tall. Use twine or string to tie the sunflower to the stake.

8. Water your sunflower often and watch it grow!

In about 1–2 months you can harvest the seeds and put them in your bird feeder. To harvest the seeds, wait until the flower heads have started to turn brown. Cut the heads, leaving a couple of inches of stem. Hang upside down by their stems to dry, in a dry, cool place. When they are dry you can easily rub out the seeds.

WETLAND BIRDS

Self-contained wetland habitats are excellent places to see a variety of birds. The view over water can be nice and clear, so take your time and watch the way wetland birds feed, nest, and interact with each other. Make notes on what you see in your Bird-Watching Notebook (see page 53). Stand on a dock or take a ride in a canoe with an adult. Use slow, quiet movements so you don't disturb the wildlife. Wildlife refuges in your area may have wetland reserves where you can watch and document annual migration cycles of the flocks of birds that visit there. Now this is really exciting! You could possibly see thousands of birds, all the same species, in one place at one time. Remember to wear clothing that is appropriate for water-watching. You might want some big rubber boots if you decide to go wading, and you may run into lots of hungry bugs and insects, so bring along some insect repellent.

MIGRATORY BIRDS

Birds migrate in North America more than anywhere else in the world. In many areas, it gets cold in the winter and food supplies decline. Migratory birds fly south in the late fall to warmer winter habitats. Then they head back north in the spring using the sun and stars as their guides. Some birds fly alone, others fly in flocks, some travel over land, and some over water. Some travel during the day, and some fly at night. They all use their innate sense of navigation to find their way home. Fifteen percent of all bird species change their habitat with the seasons. They can travel from 250 miles up to 7,000 miles!

THE V FORMATION

Migrating Geese and Ducks fly in V-shaped formations. A lead bird flies at the point of the V. Sometimes the lead bird has up to 25 other birds following him. Scientists believe that birds fly in this formation because it is a way of saving energy. The birds that follow use the air currents of the birds in front to give them an extra boost.

Discouraging Predators

Birds of prey hunt and kill small birds and rodents for food. Raccoons and skunks steal eggs out of bird nests and eat them. Snakes eat newly hatched chicks. Cats consider birds fair game. Squirrels take over bird feeders and chase birds away. To keep your backyard bird-friendly, you can discourage predators in the following ways:

◆ Do not mount man-made birdhouses or feeders in trees. Instead, put them on poles set into the ground, and place baffles on the poles.

◆ Put a bell on your cat's collar.

◆ Provide a squirrel feeder to keep squirrels away from bird feeders.

◆ Keep your birdhouses clean.

Great Blue Heron

- 🌼 Up to 50 inches long
- 🌼 Largest wading bird in North America
- 🌼 Wing span of 70 inches
- 🌼 Eats fish, small rodents, and small birds
- 🌼 Male and female look similar
- 🌼 Nests in a colony called a rookery
- 🌼 Has a loud piercing call that sounds like, *"frahnk, frahnk, frahnk"*
- 🌼 When it flies, its neck stays in the S-shaped curve

Bald Eagle

- 🌼 30 to 40 inches long
- 🌼 In 1782, it was chosen as the national bird of the United States
- 🌼 Baby is called an Eaglet; it grows up in the world's biggest nests
- 🌼 Nest can weigh up to 2 tons, and is used year after year; Eagles add branches and sticks to the nest until it gets so heavy that it falls to the ground
- 🌼 Its favorite food is fish, including salmon

Canada Goose

- 22 to 45 inches long, includes many subspecies that range in size
- Often grazes in fields on insects, grain, and grass
- Migrates south in the fall and north in the spring
- When migrating, Canadian Geese fly in a V formation
- When the flock is at rest, one or two Geese will stand guard, watching out for any dangerous predators
- Its call is a loud repeated honking sound

Mallard

- 20 to 23 inches long
- This Duck is a dabbler— this means that when it feeds, it tips head first with its tail sticking up out of the water. Many Ducks are dabblers, but some also dive down into the water instead of just tipping in
- Female is smaller than the male, does not have a green head, and is mottled brown with white tips at her tail
- Female's quack is louder than the male's

39

Belted Kingfisher

- 12 to 13 inches long
- Noticeably big head
- Lives near streams, rivers, lakes, ponds, and seacoasts
- It hovers in the air and then takes a nose dive into the water, making a big splash, to catch fish with its long, sharp beak
- Parents teach their young to fish by dropping dead fish into the water for their young to retrieve

Red-Winged Blackbird

- 7 to 9½ inches long
- Likes to build nests in marshes and damp fields
- At the end of its breeding season, it forms big flocks with other species of Blackbirds
- Grazes in the countryside during the day; at day's end, it roosts in a communal spot, often in a grove of trees
- Female is dusty brown with darker brown streaks

START YOUR OWN BIRD-WATCHING CLUB

What better way to start the day than going on a bird-watching hike with your friends!

The first thing you need to do is to tell people about your idea. A good way to do this is to make a flyer that you can mail to your friends, or hang up at your school as a poster.

Flyer or Poster:

Title: Join a Local Bird-Watching Club

Description: Hikes! Nature! Fun!

Place: (Pick a good place to meet first and then take a hike)

Time and date: (Pick a time that is not too early or late)

Suggestions on what to bring: Field guides, binoculars, notebook, colored pencils, snacks, camera, bug spray, hat

Contact Info: For questions (put your phone number)

Join my
Bird-Watching Club!
Hikes! Nature! Fun!
Time: Sunday at Noon
Place: Forest Park,
South Entrance
Bring Your
Bird-Watching Gear
More Info: 555.6564

At your meeting:

◆ Make a list of goals for your club. Maybe you would like to invite new members, volunteer at the local Audubon Society, or participate in a bird count.

◆ Discuss bird-watching etiquette (see page 12).

◆ Share any good bird-watching information or ideas. Sharing snacks is a good idea, too!

◆ Show everyone your Bird-Watching Notebook (see page 53) and plan a meeting where everyone can make their own notebook.

◆ Decide when and where your next meeting will be.

◆ Go for a hike, look for birds, have fun!

SEASHORE BIRDS

Big waves, salty air, sandy beaches, and a huge sky—what a great place to see a variety of Shorebirds, Seabirds, and Seagulls. It is not easy to identify the various species at the beach, so pay close attention to field marks. Shorebirds are cautious, stay far from humans, and are often in flocks that include different species.

Seabirds spend most of their time way out over the ocean and can be best viewed from a boat. To identify these birds, it helps to view them often and to become familiar with flight patterns, plumage (feathers), and body shape of the different species.

Seagulls are just about everywhere—on the beach, in town, at the hotel, on rooftops. Seagulls are scavengers and like to live on or near the coast, close to people so that they can eat their garbage! They also like to eat fish. There are many species of Seagulls, and it can be hard to tell them apart.

When bird-watching at the coast, be aware of the tides. Some birds like to find food at low tide; at high tide they may perch high up in a spot where you can watch them with your binoculars.

Bird-watching at the coast is a challenge, but it is a lot of fun!

Herring Gull

- 23 to 27 inches long
- One of the most common species of Seagull
- Found throughout North America, even inland near lakes and reservoirs
- Loud harsh cry sounds like *"kreeh-kreeh-kreeh"*
- While flying high over rocks or pavement, it drops shellfish onto this hard surface in order to break the shell to get at the soft meat inside
- Graceful flyer

Common Loon

- 28 to 36 inches long
- Strong legs and solid bones make it an excellent swimmer and diver; it can dive into the water as deep as 200 feet
- Common on the Great Lakes
- Big webbed feet are set back on its lower body
- The expression "crazy as a Loon" comes from its loud, yodel-like call that sounds like a strange, wailing, mournful laugh

Sooty Shearwater

- 16 to 18 inches long
- Nests on islands and along the coasts
- Nostrils are in tubes on top of its bill, called a "tuber-nose" bill; these tubes help strain the salt from the ocean water
- It rests by floating along on the water in a big flock, and from a distance this can look like a dark oily patch in the water

Brown Pelican

- 44 to 54 inches long
- Can become quite tame
- Lives in a colony and travels by flying single file over waters
- Big webbed feet
- Long bill with a big pouch that stretches from the front of its bill to its neck; pouch is used as a fish net
- Long white head and neck turns a dark brown during breeding season

Black Belly Plover

- ⚙ 10 to 13 inches long
- ⚙ Shorebird (shy bird that stays within flocks of other Shorebirds)
- ⚙ Runs along the beach, makes sudden stops, and sticks its little bill in the sand in search of insects, snails, and worms
- ⚙ Its call sounds like a clear whistle, *"Pee-oh-wee"*
- ⚙ It has a white face and black belly during breeding season, but this changes to white in the winter

Willet

- ⚙ 12 to 15 inches long
- ⚙ Pale brownish-gray color, is easily recognizable in flight by its black-and-white wing pattern
- ⚙ Likes to chatter and make a lot of noise; its voice sounds like a loud ringing *"pill-will-willet"*
- ⚙ Eats separately, but stays close to other birds; if one bird decides to visit another part of the beach, the rest will take flight and follow

BIRDBATHS

Just like you and me, birds need water to keep themselves clean, and they also like fresh water to drink. Adding a birdbath to your bird-friendly backyard is an important and fun thing to do.

You can purchase a birdbath at an outdoor home and garden store. There are many nice baths made out of cement, stone, tile, ceramic, or metal. They can be simple or fancy. Here are some important things to think about when buying or making a birdbath:

- The bowl does not have to be very deep; 3 inches is enough.
- Put some small stones on the bottom of the bowl if the surface is slippery.
- Birds like birdbaths on or close to the ground, or on pedestals.
- The bath should be made of materials that are not harmful to birds in any way (plastic, stone, suitable metal, sturdy ceramic, or cement).
- Keep it clean! Scrub all the gunk out of the birdbath when it needs it, and keep the bath filled with fresh water.

What you need:

5 rocks about the size of grapefruits
1 plastic garbage can lid
Scrub brush
Watering can or hose

What you do:

1. Clean one of the rocks and the garbage can lid with your scrub brush and some water.

2. Find a good location on the ground where you can set up your birdbath. Put it where you can easily see it. If you are concerned about predators, set the lid on a platform.

3. Set up the other 4 rocks on the ground or platform about 10 inches apart in a square.

4. Place the garbage can lid upside down on the 4 rocks, making sure the lid is stable.

5. Place the clean rock in the center of the lid to help weigh it down.

6. Use a hose or watering can to fill your birdbath.

7. Keep your birdbath filled with clean, fresh water. Keep your scrub brush handy so you can clean the bath when needed.

8. Keep an eye out for birds having some splish-splashing fun!

EASY-TO-MAKE BIRDBATH DRIPPER

Birdbaths with moving water from fountains or drippers are very popular with birds. Birds love the splash, just like taking a shower! You can make a very simple dripper and hang it over your birdbath. Hang the dripper on a tree or from a hanging pole next to your birdbath.

What you need:
A plastic gallon jug
Sturdy cord or string
Hanging pole
Small nail

What you do:

1. Clean the plastic jug and fill it with water. Put the cap on.

2. With the cord or string, hang the jug by the handle and then tie it to a limb or pole over your birdbath.

3. With the nail, punch a small hole about an inch up from the bottom of the jug, just big enough to cause a constant drip. Also punch a hole towards the top of the jug.

4. It should take about a day for your jug to empty, then you can refill it and start the drip again.

DESERT BIRDS

The desert habitat is harsh. It can be very hot during the day and nights can be very cold; water is scarce and there is limited vegetation. But don't let that stop you from bird-watching! In the deserts of the Southwest and Western United States live birds you will not see anywhere else.

The desert is a big open space and you may wonder where you should look for birds. Just like in any other habitat, you can start by looking up in the sky. It is cooler up there, and you may see a Hawk or a Vulture soaring high overhead looking for prey. Any spot that has a little shade or water is also a good place to find birds.

In the desert, as elsewhere, birds are most active in the early morning. This is especially true in the desert because of the extreme heat at midday. Don't forget your water bottle, hat, sunscreen, and binoculars!

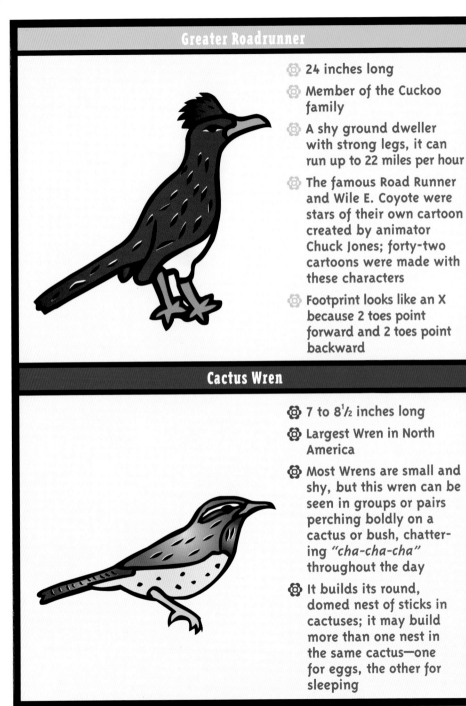

Greater Roadrunner

- 24 inches long
- Member of the Cuckoo family
- A shy ground dweller with strong legs, it can run up to 22 miles per hour
- The famous Road Runner and Wile E. Coyote were stars of their own cartoon created by animator Chuck Jones; forty-two cartoons were made with these characters
- Footprint looks like an X because 2 toes point forward and 2 toes point backward

Cactus Wren

- 7 to 8½ inches long
- Largest Wren in North America
- Most Wrens are small and shy, but this wren can be seen in groups or pairs perching boldly on a cactus or bush, chattering *"cha-cha-cha"* throughout the day
- It builds its round, domed nest of sticks in cactuses; it may build more than one nest in the same cactus—one for eggs, the other for sleeping

Red-Tailed Hawk

- 18 to 23 inches long
- Builds nest in forests, and hunts in open habitats
- Can be seen soaring over the desert looking for small rodents and reptiles to eat
- Red-Tailed Hawks help each other hunt—one makes a fake pass while the other catches the prey from behind
- Some are very dark, almost black; there are also Albino Red-Tailed Hawks—these are completely white

California Quail

- 9 to 10 inches long
- The telltale sign of a California Quail is the top-knot plume that falls over its forehead
- Female is a dull brown color
- Its call sounds like *"Chi-ca-go"*
- For most of the year it lives in groups of 10 to 20 or more, but in the spring, mated pairs are formed

Curve-Billed Thrasher

- 9 to 11 inches long
- Has a loud singing voice that sounds like a series of musical notes followed by *"whit-whit wheet"*
- Flies low to the ground and fans out its tail when it lands
- You may see it foraging on the ground looking for insects, or perched on a cactus
- Some have white wing bars

Phainopepla

- 7 to 8 inches long
- Its name means "shining robe"
- Member of the family of birds called "Silkies"
- Males are black, though you can see white wing patches when they are flying; females and juveniles are gray
- Frequently seen in desert thicket and mesquite trees eating berries and insects

YOUR BIRD-WATCHING NOTEBOOK

If you want to remember and keep records of all the different species of birds you have identified, it's a great idea to start your own Bird-Watching Notebook. Have you ever kept a diary or written about your daily life in a journal? Well, your Bird-Watching Notebook can be your bird journal, and you can fill it with your observations about all the birds that you see. The first thing you may want to put in your notebook is your Bird Diagram from page 9. This will be important when you are trying to identify a bird and need to look for its field marks.

What you need:

A sturdy spiral-bound notebook with blank white drawing paper, not too big, and easy to carry

Pencils, pens, markers, colored pencils

Pencil sharpener

Eraser

Envelope, a size that fits on the notebook's inside back cover

Tape or glue stick

Scissors

Stickers, old magazines (optional)

What you do:

1. Make a label for the cover of your notebook. I have taped mine on the cover with extra-wide clear tape, right in the center. (I also added a few stickers.) You can label and decorate your cover any way you want.

2. Write your contact information inside the front cover (name, phone number, address) just in case you leave your notebook somewhere or lose it. You may get lucky and it will be returned.

3. Tie the top of a pencil with string, then tie the other end of the string to the top of the spiral coil. Now you'll never have to look for a pencil when using your notebook! Make sure you leave enough string so that the pencil is easy to use. Store it in the spiral coil.

4. On the inside back cover of your notebook, tape or glue an envelope so you have a place to store leaves, feathers, photos, separate notes, and articles. Make sure the envelope is the right size for your notebook, and make sure the flap is facing out towards you. You do not want to permanently close this flap—secure your items inside by simply tucking it in.

When you spot and identify a bird, use your notebook to document this information:

1. Time, date, place, and weather
2. The bird's appearance, field marks, color, size, and shape
3. The bird's behavior
4. If the bird is vocal, a description of its call or song
5. A sketch/drawing of the bird and surroundings

You can add some of this information later, when you are at home, so that when you are "out in the field" you can spend most of your time watching the birds. I use one page per bird, but you can set up your notebook however it works well for you. When you have filled this notebook, you can start a new one and call it "Volume 2"!

SKETCHING BIRDS

Ok, now it is time to bring out the colored pencils and magic markers! Go ahead and sketch your little heart out. Your drawing does not have to be perfect, it just helps to remind you of what you've seen. When sketching birds, it is nice if they stay put for a little while. It also helps when starting out on a sketch to outline your bird in a series of shapes that make up the whole bird. Its head can be a small oval, and its body can be a bigger oval. Its beak can be a triangle shape, and so on. Keep adding until you've got the whole bird. Then you can add color and shading. Hey, this is fun!

Here are some other uses for your notebook:

1. Collect feathers, leaves, photos, and interesting articles. Put these in your envelope for storage, and sometime later you can tape or glue them to the appropriate page in your notebook.

2. Make bird lists. You may want to have a few pages in your notebook devoted just to lists.

Here are some lists that are fun for a bird-watcher to make:

◆ **Yard list: a list of all the birds you have seen in your backyard.**

◆ **City or state list: a list of all the birds you have seen in one city or state.**

◆ **Year list: a list of all the birds you have seen in one calendar year.**

◆ **Life list: a list of all the birds you have ever seen and identified in your entire life!**

FOR THE LOVE OF BIRDS

The more time you spend bird-watching, the better birder you will become. Watch our feathered friends from a distance; do not handle them or disturb their nests; do not chase them or destroy their habitat in any way. Go bird-watching as often as you can, in as many places as you can, and your experiences will be filled with surprises and enjoyment. It is incredibly exciting to spot a Hawk soaring in the sky. Hawks float and glide with the wind currents, and dive with a power and precision that is awe-inspiring. Wow! Did you see that? A dance with the clouds.

JOHN JAMES AUDUBON

 John James Audubon was a great bird artist. His goal was to make a painting of every American bird. From 1819 to 1826, Audubon traveled all over the United States, observing birds and creating paintings for the book *Birds of America*. This book has 435 hand-colored engravings that depict 1,065 species of birds in their natural habitats. These images are life-size, making this a very large book. Audubon painted the birds and another artist, Joseph Robert Mason, painted the backgrounds. These are some of the most beautiful and famous images of birds you will ever see.

THE AUDUBON SOCIETY

The Audubon Society is a national organization named after John James Audubon. Its mission is to conserve and restore natural ecosystems and habitats for birds and other wildlife. There are community-based nature centers and chapters all over the United States. These centers focus on scientific and educational programs. They argue for areas that sustain important bird populations. These centers encourage people of all ages and backgrounds to have positive conservation experiences (see Websites, page 63).

ROGER TORY PETERSON

Roger Tory Peterson was a world-renowned and much honored naturalist. He loved nature and animals, and had a special passion for birds. He was an artist, writer, photographer, filmmaker, educator, environmentalist, and conservationist. He wrote, edited, and illustrated many popular field guide books, and came up with the practical use of "field marks" (see page 9) as an identification system.

STATE BIRDS

Alabama: **Northern Flicker**

Alaska: **Willow Ptarmigan**

Arizona: **Cactus Wren**

Arkansas: **Northern Mockingbird**

California: **California Quail**

Colorado: **Lark Bunting**

Connecticut: **American Robin**

Delaware: **Blue Hen Chicken**

Florida: **Northern Mockingbird**

Georgia: **Brown Thrasher**

Hawaii: **Hawaiian Goose**

Idaho: **Mountain Bluebird**

Illinois: **Northern Cardinal**

Indiana: **Northern Cardinal**

Iowa: **American Goldfinch**

Kansas: **Western Meadowlark**

Kentucky: **Northern Cardinal**

Louisiana: **Brown Pelican**

Maine: **Black-Capped Chickadee**

Maryland: **Baltimore Oriole**

Massachusetts: **Black-Capped Chickadee**

Michigan: **American Robin**

Minnesota: **Common Loon**

Mississippi: **Northern Mockingbird**

Missouri: **Eastern Bluebird**

Montana: **Western Meadowlark**

Nebraska: **Western Meadowlark**

Nevada: **Mountain Bluebird**

New Hampshire: **Purple Finch**

New Jersey: American Goldfinch

New Mexico: **Greater Roadrunner**

New York: **Eastern Bluebird**

North Carolina: **Northern Cardinal**

North Dakota: **Western Meadowlark**

Ohio: **Northern Cardinal**

Oklahoma: **Scissor-Tailed Flycatcher**

Oregon: **Western Meadowlark**

Pennsylvania: **Ruffed Grouse**

Rhode Island: **Rhode Island Red Chicken**

South Carolina: **Carolina Wren**

South Dakota: **Ring-Necked Pheasant**

Tennessee: **Northern Mockingbird**

Texas: **Northern Mockingbird**

Utah: **California Gull**

Vermont: **Hermit Thrush**

Virginia: **Northern Cardinal**

Washington: **American Goldfinch**

West Virginia: **Northern Cardinal**

Wisconsin: **American Robin**

Wyoming: **Western Meadowlark**

WHAT DO YOU DO IF YOU FIND A BABY BIRD?

If you find a baby bird on the ground, you should leave it alone. Its parent is probably somewhere near, and will return. Watch the baby bird from a distance, and if no parent shows up after an hour, try to find the nest that the baby may have fallen from. It's not a good idea to handle a baby bird, or touch their nests. This is not because the parents will abandon it after you have touched it, but because you could leave your scent on the baby, which could lead predators to this bird and its nest. It is against the law to handle or own native wild birds unless you have a permit.

Call a bird rehabilitation center in your area. You can find one near you by calling your local bird club, the Audubon Society, or a veterinarian. You can also get information from the International Wildlife Rehabilitation Council or Wildlife International (see Websites, page 63). It may take time to get to a wildlife rehabilitator and they may instruct you to keep the baby bird warm by making a nest for it in a small box with shredded paper and pieces of cloth. You also could set up a lightbulb over the nest to give the baby bird some added heat. The rehabilitation center may also have instructions for feeding.

IT'S A BIRD'S LIFE

What can you do to make life better for birds? Well, you have already started if you have made your backyard bird friendly by adding bird boxes, a birdbath, a bird feeder, or a garden. You can also:

◆ Join or start your own Bird-Watching Club, and go hiking with friends in your favorite bird-watching areas. Share information about birds.

◆ Contact your nearest Audubon Society chapter. You can help protect bird habitats and species that are becoming extinct by finding out what is going on in your community.

◆ If you are old enough, volunteer at a bird rehabilitation center, National Wildlife Refuge, or a state or local park, and get some hands-on experience.

◆ Find out about local and national "bird counts," and be a participant. A "bird count" is just what it sounds like—you count birds for a certain number of hours in a specified place. A famous one is called "The Christmas Bird Count," and these results are sent to the National Audubon Society.

Excellent Bird Websites

www.audubon.org

www.birdwatchersdigest.com

www.americanbirding.org

www.iwrc-online.org

www.wildlife-international.org

Excellent Bird Books

Bird Watching for Dummies, Bill Thomson, III

The Backyard Birdhouse Book, Rene and Christyna Laubach

Everything You Never Learned About Birds, Rebecca Rupp

The FeederWatcher's Guide to Bird Feeding, Barker & Griggs

Bird Supply Websites

For sunflower seeds: www.burpee.com

For pinecones: www.pinecones.com

Collect them all!

Available at bookstores or directly from
GIBBS SMITH, PUBLISHER
1.800.748.5439/www.gibbs-smith.com